TO START WITH...

HERE'S A LITTLE DIAGRAM TO SHOW HOW MUCH EVERYBODY ON THE PLANET WANTS TO BE HAPPY!

...AND THE ANSWER IS:
YES!
SUPER BRAINY
BOUNCY HAIR
SHINING EYES
BEAMING SMILE
GOOD SENSE OF HUMOUR
ENERGETIC
MISS HAPPY
DANCING FEET
PROOF

EVEN WHEN THINGS AREN'T GOING SO WELL...

EVERYBODY CAN LEARN WHAT TRUE HAPPINESS IS!

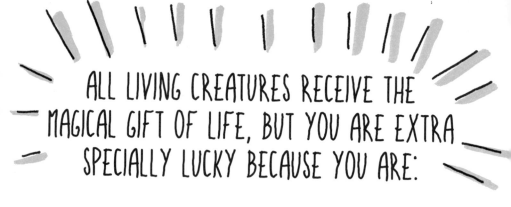

ALL LIVING CREATURES RECEIVE THE MAGICAL GIFT OF LIFE, BUT YOU ARE EXTRA SPECIALLY LUCKY BECAUSE YOU ARE:

100% HUMAN

AND SO YOU GET ALL THE SPECIAL PRIVILEGES RESERVED FOR HUMANS

LIKE, FOR EXAMPLE:

. . . .

WEARING NAIL VARNISH

I AM RICH!

GETTING POCKET MONEY

BEFORE | AFTER

CHOOSING YOUR HAIRSTYLE

BURP

PFFFT

STUFFING YOURSELF WITH PEANUT BUTTER

THINKING ABOUT YOUR FUTURE JOB

LION TAMER

YOU ARE A MORON!

USE YOUR LITTLE BRAIN TO THINK ABOUT ALL THE OTHER ADVANTAGES TOO!

HERE ARE A FEW EXAMPLES OF
LIVING THINGS, BUT NOT HUMAN
BEINGS, WHO ARE A LOT LESS
LUCKY THAN YOU:

NO FRIENDS ON
FACEBOOK

WILL NEVER KNOW WHAT LOVE IS

Oh woe is me!
What a
miserable life!

CAN'T SEE A PSYCHIATRIST WHEN
THINGS AREN'T GOING WELL

HAS NEVER BEEN AWAY ON
HOLIDAY IN ITS LIFE

HAS NEVER SEEN THE SEA

I'M STARVING!
EATS THE SAME THING EVERY DAY, EVEN AT CHRISTMAS
CAN'T HAVE PIZZAS DELIVERED TO ITS HOME
HAS TO HUNT FOR FOOD
WILL NEVER DISCOVER THE FANTASTIC TASTE OF CHEESECAKE

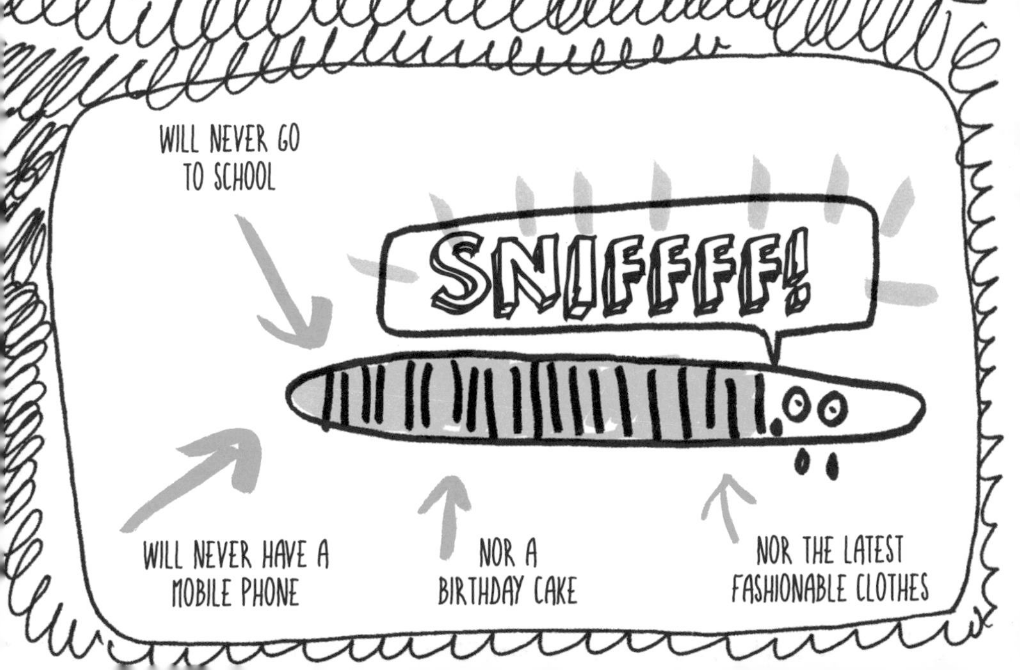
WILL NEVER GO TO SCHOOL
SNIFFFF!
WILL NEVER HAVE A MOBILE PHONE
NOR A BIRTHDAY CAKE
NOR THE LATEST FASHIONABLE CLOTHES

MORE

CAN'T WEAR A COAT
TO KEEP WARM IN WINTER

* (TRANSLATION — I'M ABSOLUTELY FROZEN!
GET ME A TICKET TO HAWAII, QUICK!)

* BRRRRRRRR!
BRRRRRRRR!

DOESN'T KNOW HOW
TO PUT UP A TENT

ONLY HAS ONE PAIR
OF UNDERPANTS, AND
THEY'RE MADE OF FUR

GOOD NEWS: YOU CONTROL YOUR LIFE!

IT'S UP TO YOU TO THINK CAREFULLY AND FILL IT WITH EVERYTHING YOU LOVE TO MAKE IT EXTRAORDINARY.

EXAMPLE 1

A TINY SHRIVELLED UP LIFE, FULL OF SAD AND BORING THINGS

UGH! I DON'T WANT THAT! YOU MUST BE JOKING!

EXAMPLE 2

A LIFE FULL OF HAPPINESS, LAUGHTER AND FUN

YUMMY! I WANT THAT!

THE BAD NEWS: HAPPINESS DOESN'T JUST FALL OUT OF THE SKY. (WHAT A SHAME!)

24-HOUR HAPPINESS DELIVERY SERVICE

PARCELS FULL OF GOODIES AND DELIGHT

A HUMAN BEING SQUASHED BY TOO MUCH HAPPINESS (YES, IT DOES HAPPEN)

I WANT SOME!

ME TOO!

Advert

DEAR, SUPER-KIND READER,
IF YOU DON'T UNDERSTAND ANYTHING
IN THIS BOOK, I CAN COME

TO YOUR HOUSE AND EXPLAIN

for the modest sum of

£1,000,000

~~MONEY GRABBING AND NOT TO BE TRUSTED~~

QUALIFIED INTERNATIONAL HAPPINESS SPECIALIST

~~WANTS TO FLEECE YOUR PARENTS~~

ENDLESSLY PATIENT (EVEN WITH REALLY STUPID PEOPLE)

Personal happiness

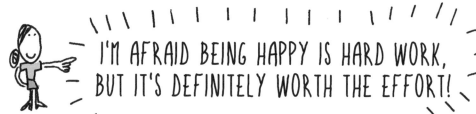

I'M AFRAID BEING HAPPY IS HARD WORK, BUT IT'S DEFINITELY WORTH THE EFFORT!

TAKE YOUR OATH HERE:

 1 PLACE YOUR LEFT HAND ON YOUR HEART.

 2 CLOSE YOUR EYES (READ ALL THE INSTRUCTIONS FIRST).

JUST SAY YOUR OATH IN YOUR TINY HEAD, YOU SLOBBERY SAUSAGE!

THIS OATH IS TOTALLY USELESS! WHAT ABOUT WORMS WHO HAVEN'T GOT ANY HANDS?

MAKE SURE YOU ALWAYS REALISE WHEN YOU ARE HAPPY!

VERY IMPORTANT!

PHILOSOPHICAL BUTTERFLY →

REMEMBER! THE MORE YOU'RE AWARE OF YOUR HAPPINESS, THE GREATER IT IS!

'COS HOW RUBBISH WOULD IT BE TO BE HAPPY AND NOT EVEN REALISE IT!

HAPPINESS MAKES YOU FEEL LIKE YOU CAN FLY, FLY, FLY...

YAHOO!
CHEEP! CHEEP!

WOO HOO!
CHIRP! CHIRP!

CLOUD LAYER

DARLING, WHO ARE THOSE TWO SHOW-OFFS WEARING ONLY UNDERPANTS WHO THINK THEY'RE BUDGIES?

THEY'RE SUPER HAPPY HUMANS, WHO FLOAT PAST FROM TIME TO TIME...

EARTH

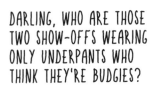

HAPPINESS CAN MAKE YOU SMILE LIKE AN IDIOT.

 **A** WHAT YOU LOOK LIKE MOST OF THE TIME

 **B** AFTER AN AWESOME PIECE OF NEWS

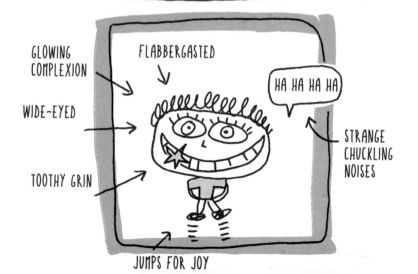

HAPPINESS MAKES YOU GLOW.

IT FILLS YOU WITH AMAZING ENERGY.

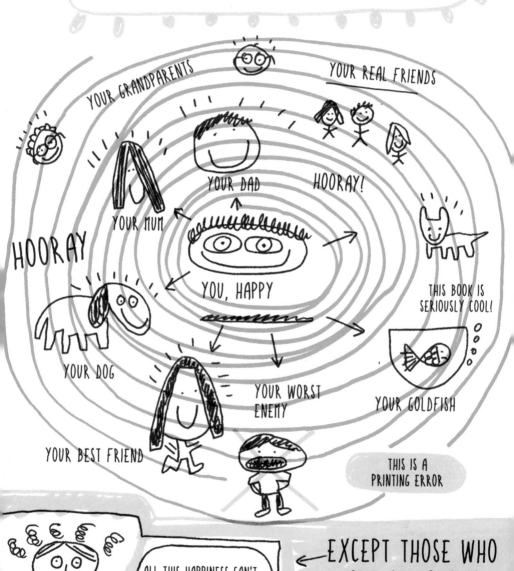

HAPPINESS IS INFINITE: THERE'S ALWAYS ENOUGH FOR EVERYONE...

PROOF

WHAT'S THE DIFFERENCE BETWEEN A HUGE CREAM CAKE AND HAPPINESS?

A

B

HAPPINESS

EVEN WHEN YOU THINK HAPPINESS IS PLAYING HIDE-AND-SEEK WITH YOU... IT'S NEVER FAR AWAY!

DON'T WORRY!

pile of yucky things which sometimes happen in life

HAPPINESS HIDDEN AWAY, BUT YOU'LL FIND IT AGAIN VERY SOON.

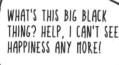

WHAT'S THIS BIG BLACK THING? HELP, I CAN'T SEE HAPPINESS ANY MORE!

QUIZ

FIND THE 2 UNHAPPY PEOPLE ON THIS PAGE WHO HAVEN'T BEEN LUCKY ENOUGH TO READ THIS AWESOME BOOK.

TOO EASY! DOES SHE THINK YOU'RE AN IDIOT?

DRAW YOURSELF SWIMMING IN HAPPINESS!

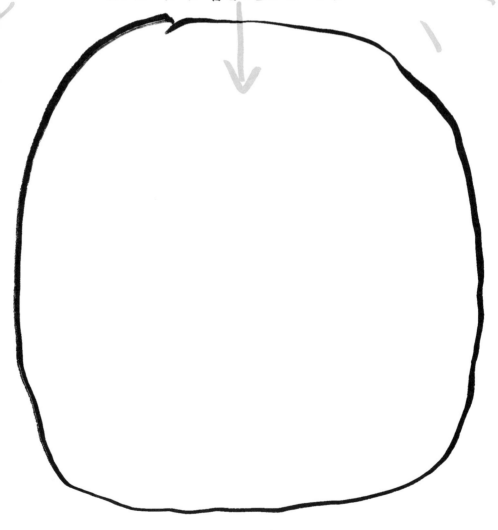

 BE CAREFUL NOT TO DROWN!

WATCH OUT! THE RIGHT-HAND PAGE IS VERY SCARY!!!

HELLOOO, READER!
I'M YOUR LUCKY STAR;
LOOK AT ME EVERY TIME
YOU NEED SOME LUCK!

EXAMPLES

TO PASS A TEST WHICH YOU HAVEN'T REVISED FOR AT ALL.	SO NOBODY WILL NOTICE YOU'VE DONE SOMETHING STUPID.
TO IMPRESS THE GIRL OR BOY OF YOUR DREAMS AT A PARTY.	TO GET THE PART YOU WANT IN THE SCHOOL PLAY.

DO YOU THINK THIS STAR REALLY HAS MAGICAL POWERS? OR IS IT A LOAD OF NONSENSE?

OF COURSE IT HAS! I LOOKED AT IT AND I HAD CAVIAR FOR SCHOOL DINNER, I GOT 21 OUT OF 20 IN AN EXAM AND THE BEST-LOOKING GUY IN THE WHOLE WORLD TOLD ME HE LOVES ME!

TURN OVER QUICKLY TO DISCOVER THE BASIC RULES OF BEING HAPPY!

→

RULE No. 1

SPREAD LOVE ALL AROUND

AMONG THE PEOPLE THAT SURROUND YOU

AND IN EVERYTHING YOU DO (YOUR HOMEWORK FOR EXAMPLE)

↑

ARE YOU MAD?

BONKERS!

RULE No. 2

ALWAYS LOOK ON THE BRIGHT SIDE OF LIFE.

LIKE HIM:

I MAY BE A WORM, BUT AT LEAST I DON'T SPEND MEGA BUCKS ON NAIL VARNISH, RINGS, TRAINERS OR JEANS THAT'LL BE OUT OF FASHION IN 3 DAYS TIME.
GET IT?

MINI QUIZ

GUESS WHICH OF THESE 2 PEOPLE IS BEST-QUALIFIED TO BE HAPPY?

ATTITUDE (A)

ARGHH!
A COMPLETE MORON ONLY LEFT ME A TINY BIT OF DRIED-UP PIZZA FOR DINNER! BOO HOO! LIFE STINKS! THE WHOLE WORLD IS AGAINST ME! I'M GOING TO DIE OF STARVATION!!!

ATTITUDE (B)

WOO HOO, BRILLIANT!!! A KIND, GENEROUS PERSON LEFT ME LOADS OF DELICIOUS PIZZA! YUM YUM! I'M JUST SOOO LUCKY!

BURPPPPPP
OOPS! EXCUSE ME!

RULE No. 3

ENCOURAGE FRIENDSHIPS

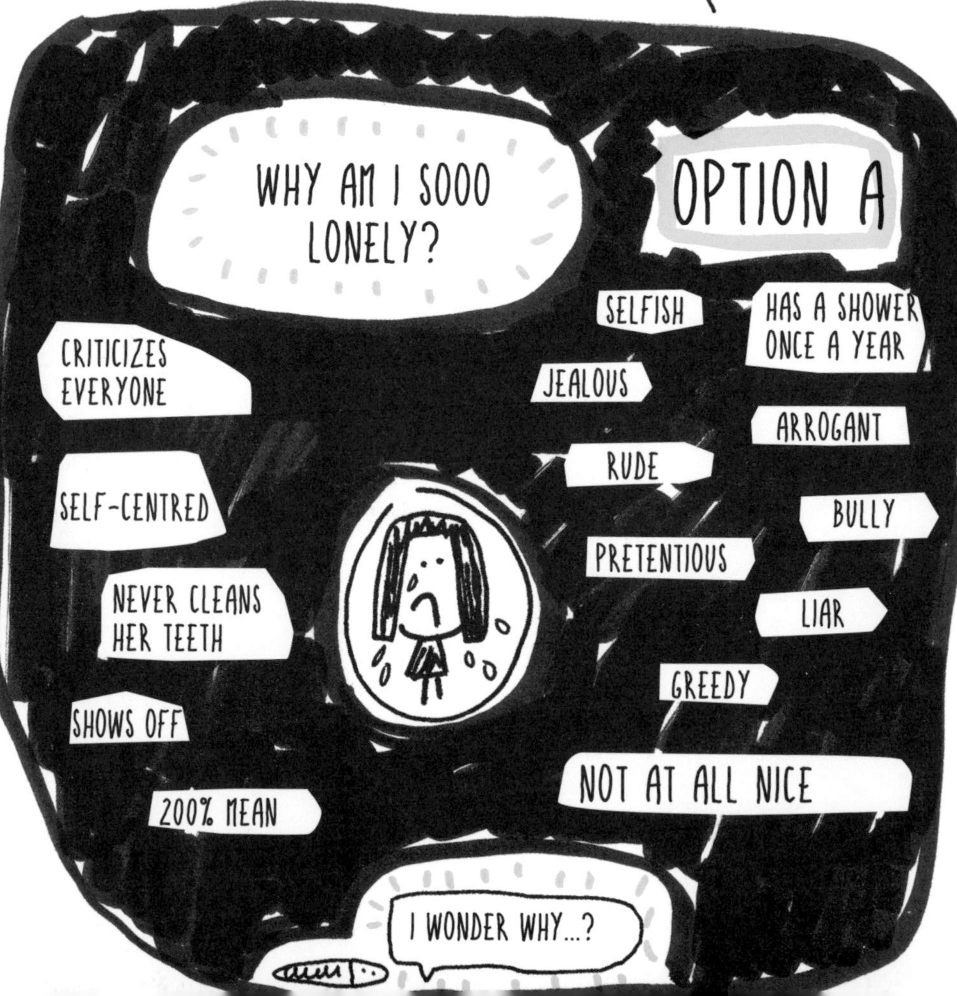

RULE No. 4

FREEDOM IS ESSENTIAL FOR HAPPINESS

(1) EVEN IF YOU SOMETIMES *FEEL* LIKE YOU'RE IN PRISON...

2 AT LEAST YOU'RE FREE TO THINK WHAT YOU WANT.

PLEASE, GOD, LET THEM SUDDENLY COLLAPSE WITH INDIGESTION FROM EATING GREENS, SO I CAN LIVE MY LIFE HOW I WANT.

THE CHILDREN'S LIBERATION GOD

3 YOU HAVE THE RIGHT TO SAY WHAT YOU WANT (BUT CONSIDER THE CONSEQUENCES CAREFULLY).

YUCK!

STEAMED COURGETTES ARE DISGUSSSSSTING! ARE YOU TRYING TO KILL ME?

4 AND IN A FEW YEARS' TIME YOU'LL BE COMPLETELY FREE.

YOUR DESTINY

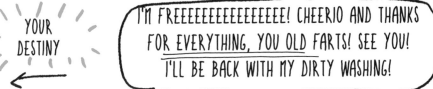

I'M FREEEEEEEEEEEEEEEEE! CHEERIO AND THANKS FOR EVERYTHING, YOU OLD FARTS! SEE YOU! I'LL BE BACK WITH MY DIRTY WASHING!

A FAREWELL SPEECH WHICH SHOWS YOUR PARENTS HOW GRATEFUL YOU ARE FOR THE HAPPY CHILDHOOD THEY GAVE YOU (I HOPE)

RULE No. 5

DOWN WITH VIOLENCE! PEACE RULES!

WATCH OUT! SPECIAL GUEST STAR!

RAYS OF LIGHT

LEVITATION

THE GREAT MAN OF PEACE HAS COME SPECIALLY FROM PEACELAND TO WRITE SOMETHING IN THIS BOOK.

HEY BUTTERFLY, WHO'S THE BALD GUY WITH THE GIRL'S DRESS ???

????

I'VE GOT NO IDEA!

100% FORBIDDEN!

> HEY, FISH FACE! YOU'RE NOT MY FRIEND ANY MORE! I'M GONNA THROW CAKE AT YOU, STEAL YOUR HAMSTER AND MAKE YOUR LIFE HELL, SO GO ON AND CALL YOUR MUM!

GRRRR GRRRR

> HELP! MUUUM!

200% RECOMMENDED

GRRRR THIS WALLY IS REALLY GETTING UP MY NOSE!

ARGH! WHAT A PRAT!

ALWAYS MAKE A HUGE EFFORT, EVEN IF IT'S A STRUGGLE SOMETIMES!

A MIRACULOUS LITTLE RITUAL TO CARRY OUT EVERY SINGLE DAY.

READ THE OPPOSITE PAGE IN A MIRROR EACH MORNING BEFORE YOU CLEAN YOUR TEETH.

⟶

IN THE MORNING

RIGHT: I'VE GOT MY FALSE TEETH, SOME TOOTHPASTE, A TOOTHBRUSH AND A LITTLE MIRROR, SO I CAN TRY THIS LITTLE EXPERIMENT TOO...

HAVE AN AWESOMELY WONDERFUL DAY DUDE!

THE SAME EVENING

OH WOW AND SUPER WOW! IT REALLY WORKS! I GOT A NEW GIRLFRIEND AND I WON THE LOTTERY...

£1, 000, 000

AND HERE
ARE A
FEW HINTS
ON HOW
TO BE
EVEN

HAPPIER
━━7

BELIEVE IN YOURSELF 100%

SUPER POWERS!

NO DOUBTS WHATSOEVER

YESSS, I CAN DO ANYTHING! WHERE THERE'S A WILL THERE'S A WAY!

HAVE CONFIDENCE IN YOURSELF

BUT NOT IN HIM.

VERY FIERCE DOG

ACCEPT YOURSELF FOR WHAT YOU ARE.

I'M SUPER GOOD-LOOKING, SUPER-INTELLIGENT AND EXCEPTIONALLY-GIFTED, BUT VERY MODEST. I'VE GOT A PERFECT BODY, I'M INCREDIBLY BRIGHT WITH A SENSE OF HUMOUR TO DIE FOR... IN FACT, I'M JUST SOOO HAPPY TO BE ME!

BUT REMEMBER, THIS DOESN'T MEAN YOU DON'T HAVE ANY FAULTS AT ALL!

CHOOSE YOUR FRIENDS CAREFULLY!

 **A** AN EXCELLENT CHOICE:

GET AWAY FROM THIS DREADFUL MORON RIGHTAWAY!

OH YES, BY THE WAY CAN YOU LEND ME A HUNDRED QUID? HAVE YOU GOT A GIFT VOUCHER YOU CAN GIVE ME?

IT'S STRANGE, YOU LOOK JUST LIKE A REALLY UNCOOL GIRL I KNOW.

YOU LOOK REALLY DAFT WITH THAT HAIRCUT. YOU REMIND ME OF MY COUSIN'S DOG!

I CAN'T COME TO YOUR PARTY, I'M ALREADY GOING TO ONE. BY THE WAY CAN I BORROW YOUR JEANS?

NO, I NEVER ANSWER THE PHONE WHEN YOU NEED ME. I HAVEN'T GOT TIME!!!

YOU KNOW WHAT, SOMETHING REALLY BAD JUST HAPPENED TO ME...

YOUR SUPPOSED 'FRIEND'

YOU GET THE PICTURE, RIGHT?

BE GENEROUS AND SHARE WITH YOUR FRIENDS!

EXAMPLE (ALTHOUGH IT'S A BIT OTT REALLY)

MAKE AN EFFORT!
(EVEN IF IT'S HARD).

HEY READER, DO YOU WANT A BIT OF MY CHEWING GUM? ← A VERY SMALL SACRIFICE

PLEASE LET HIM REFUSE, DEAR GOD! — SLIGHT TRACE OF SELFISHNESS

BLATANT LIE

GO ON, I REALLY WANT YOU TO TAKE IT!

FORCED SMILE →

ARM READY TO SPRING BACK QUICKLY

YOU'RE SUCH A SAINT →

SCALE OF HAPPINESS

HEAVEN ON EARTH

CONGRATULATIONS

- ALWAYS POSITIVE!
- ALWAYS READY TO MAKE THINGS BETTER.
- HAPPY AND ENERGETIC.

- DESPITE A ROUGH START, MAKES A CONSCIOUS EFFORT TO BE HAPPIER EVERY DAY.
- WELL DONE!
- WILL REACH THE NEXT LEVEL VERY SOON.

WELL DONE, KEEP IT UP!

KEEP TRYING
HELL ON EARTH
GRRRR!
IT'S ALL BAAAAAAAD!
• STILL HASN'T UNDERSTOOD THE BASIC RULES ABOUT BEING HAPPY.
• NEVER CONTENT.
• PESSIMISTIC.
• ALWAYS MOANING.
• NEGATIVE.
GET IT?

GET RID OF FEAR AND SHYNESS IN 4 EASY STAGES.

STAGE NO. 1 → THINK OF SOMETHING YOU'D LOVE TO DO BUT ARE TOO SCARED.

STAGE NO. 2 → REPEAT 2,500 TIMES IN FRONT OF A MIRROR: ↓

EASY PEASY!
I CAN DO IT!
I REALLY CAN!
IT'S SOOOOOOO SIMPLE!

COOL RELAXED ATTITUDE →

WHISTLING

SMILE!

HANDS IN POCKETS →

CLOSE YOUR EYES AND IMAGINE
YOU'RE A SUPER-HERO!

100% EFFICIENT
SELF-PERSUASION

I'M THE GUY WHO ISN'T SCARED OF ANYTHING! I'VE GOT SUPER-HUMAN POWERS!!! NANANANANA!

STAGE NO. 4 → THEN... JUMP STRAIGHT IN WITH BOTH FEET!

EXAMPLE ON NEXT PAGE

← SEE PREVIOUS PAGE

GO FOR IT! GO ON! YOU'VE GOT NOTHING TO LOSE!

 ← SLOBBERY FAN

EXAMPLE: IN THE PLAYGROUND

YOU, TRANSFORMED INTO A
BLOCK OF PURE CONFIDENCE

TOTALLY-OUT-OF-YOUR-LEAGUE
MOST POPULAR GIRL IN SCHOOL

REACTION A

REACTION B

HELLO GIRL I LIKE, HOW ABOUT COMING TO THE CINEMA WITH ME ON WEDNESDAY?

??

GODDESS

FASHIONISTA

INCREDIBLE

10.01AM → POSSIBLE REACTION NO. 1

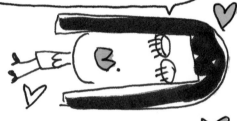

BEAMING WITH PRIDE

AHHHH AT LAST HE'S MADE UP HIS MIND! I'VE BEEN WAITING FOR THIS PRECIOUS MOMENT SINCE NURSERY SCHOOL...

GODDESS PASSED OUT WITH HAPPINESS

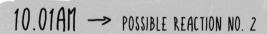

10.01AM → POSSIBLE REACTION NO. 2

GREAT...

HOW DARE YOU SPEAK TO ME, YOU STUPID BOY!

BUT AT LEAST YOU WON'T HAVE ANY REGRETS!

STOP THINKING THAT THE GRASS IS ALWAYS GREENER...

THE WHATDOYOUCALLITS GO TO HAWAII EVERY WEEKEND, THEY'VE GOT 4 LIMOS, THEY HAVE CHIPS WITH EVERY MEAL, THEY GO TO BED AT 3AM AND WHEN THEY POO IT SMELLS REALLY NICE!

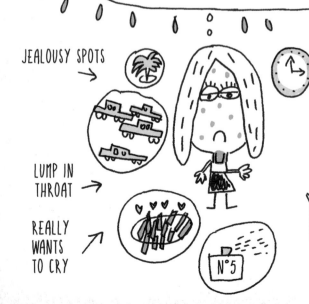

JEALOUSY SPOTS →

LUMP IN THROAT →

REALLY WANTS TO CRY ↗

IT'S A MESS AT OUR HOUSE!

WE ALWAYS EAT ORGANIC FOOD!

MUM AND DAD MAKE US LISTEN TO THE TALKING BITS ON THE RADIO!

N°5

CLOSE YOUR EYES AND THINK ABOUT EVERYTHING THAT'S REALLY GREAT IN YOUR LIFE!

IF YOU'RE A WORM...

1 NO DIRTY PANTS AND SOCKS TO PUT IN THE LAUNDRY BASKET.

2 DON'T HAVE TO KISS BRISTLY OR SMELLY OLD PEOPLE.

3 DON'T HAVE TO WORK.

4 WILL NEVER HAVE TO WEAR A BRACE ON MY TEETH.

5 AND THERE ARE LOADS MORE I'VE FORGOTTEN.

WOO HOO!
MY LIFE IS JUST HEAVEN!

DREAM PAGE

BE INQUISITIVE!
EXPLORE, DISCOVER AND UNDERSTAND THE MYSTERIOUS, MAGICAL WORLD AROUND YOU...

FOR EXAMPLE: MODERN ART

MASTERPIECE FROM THE MUSEUM OF MODERN ART

OH REALLY? ARE YOU SURE IT ISN'T A PIECE OF DOG POO?

SO IF I PAINT THE SAME THING, WILL I GET 300 MILLION POUNDS?

DON'T LISTEN TO THE DREADFUL SPOILSPORTS
(A VERY DANGEROUS SPECIES).

IT'S GOING TO SNOW

NO FUTURE

THE WORLD WILL DEFINITELY END ON 34TH DECEMBER!

THIS BOOK IS SERIOUSLY STUPID! DO YOU REALLY FIND IT FUNNY?

UNLESS YOU GIVE ME ALL YOUR MONEY

GREEDY GURU

I WANT TO BE A ROCK STAR!

OH COME ON, ACTUALLY GET REAL! YOU'LL NEVER MAKE IT, SO WHY BOTHER TRYING!

YOU'LL END UP POOR, UNEDUCATED, OUT-OF-WORK, OVERWEIGHT AND ABANDONED IN A STINKY DUSTBIN!

RUBBISH CLAIRVOYANT →

THE ANSWER

SUPER EARPLUGS©

THESE EARPLUGS WILL STOP YOU HEARING ALL THE WORDS WHICH COULD SHATTER YOUR DREAMS.

HE MUST TAKE ME FOR
A REAL NINCOMPOOP!!

DOES HE THINK HE'S
THE ONLY CHILD IN
THE WORLD?

I'M GOING TO BOX HIS EARS,
THAT'S ALL HE DESERVES!!!

YET ANOTHER STUPID HUMAN
WHO HASN'T UNDERSTOOD THAT
HAVING MILLIONS OF USELESS
THINGS DOESN'T MAKE YOU HAPPY?

IT'S ENOUGH TO MAKE YOUR
CHRISTMAS TREE COME OUT IN SPOTS!

P.S. IF YOU
DON'T GIVE ME
EVERYTHING ON
THE LIST, I'LL
THROW A
TANTRUM!

WHAT'S MORE, ALL
THOSE PRESENTS POLLUTE
THE PLANET.

SUPER-CLEVER TALKING CHRISTMAS TREE

DON'T TRY TO BE LIKE EVERYONE ELSE.

IF YOU DO, LOOK WHAT HORRIBLE THING MIGHT HAPPEN AS YOU COME OUT OF SCHOOL

INSTEAD DECIDE WHAT MAKES YOU REALLY HAPPY AND JUST DO IT!

SPENDING ALL MY LIFE IN BED WATCHING DVDS AND EATING NUTELLA® STRAIGHT FROM THE JAR WITH MY FINGER WHILE MAKING HOAX PHONE CALLS!

LIFE'S A DREAM!

LA LA LA!

TOTAL BLISS.

WHY NOT MAKE A LIST OF THE
MOST INTELLIGENT ACTIVITIES
THAT MAKE YOU SUPER HAPPY?

I'VE GOT IT!
I LOVE WEARING FANCY DRESS!

AND SKATEBOARDING
ROCKS!

NOT TRUE! YOU BIG FIBBER!

NEWLY-STYLED HAIR →

← LAYABOUT

LAZYBONES →

DISCO SHOES →

ENJOY THE GREAT OUTDOORS!

SHORT GREEN MESSAGE

GO DIVING

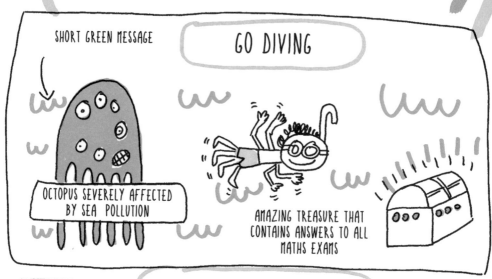

OCTOPUS SEVERELY AFFECTED BY SEA POLLUTION

AMAZING TREASURE THAT CONTAINS ANSWERS TO ALL MATHS EXAMS

LOOK AT THE SKY, THE STARS AND CLOUD FORMATIONS

HEADTEACHER OF YOUR SCHOOL

JAR OF NUTELLA®

TOO PRETTY

PFFFFTTT →

SO WHAT? IT'S ONLY NATURAL!

STEADY ON NOW, THIS IS A
CHILDREN'S BOOK YOU KNOW!!!

DON'T SPEND YOUR LIFE
GLUED TO A SCREEN!

DON'T SPEND YOUR LIFE
GLUED TO A SCREEN!

DON'T SPEND YOUR LIFE
GLUED TO A SCREEN!

DON'T SPEND YOUR LIFE
GLUED TO A SCREEN!

YOU'LL TURN INTO A
MEGA-STUPID COUCH POTATO.

I'VE REPEATED MYSELF TO GET MY
MESSAGE ACROSS, PLUS IT MEANS I DON'T HAVE
TO DRAW ANYTHING ON THIS PAGE! HA HA HA!

TRY TO BE WITH REAL PEOPLE IN THIS WONDERFUL REAL LIFE!

ADVANTAGES OF REAL PEOPLE

YOU CAN TOUCH THEM

KISS THEM

HOLD THEIR HANDS

TICKLE THEM

HUG THEM

WHISPER SWEET NOTHINGS IN THEIR EARS

KNOW IF THEY'RE COLD OR HOT

FEEL THEIR SKIN

STICK YOUR FINGER UP THEIR NOSE
PINCH THEIR BOTTOM

SMELL THEIR PERFUME

THE BEST THING : THEY'RE ALWAYS THERE, EVEN WHEN YOUR COMPUTER AND YOUR TV HAVE BROKEN DOWN!

REAL LIFE IS JUST TOO WONDERFUL!

A LITTLE AERIAL VIEW

SATELLITE VIEW OF THE EARTH

(A) BEFORE THIS BOOK WAS PUBLISHED

(B) AFTER THIS BOOK WAS PUBLISHED

THE NUMBER OF SUPER MEGA HAPPY CHILDREN IN THE WORLD

WOW!

AFTER THIS BOOK
WAS PUBLISHED

Ⓑ

Ⓐ

BEFORE THIS BOOK
WAS PUBLISHED

* LAUGH AS MUCH AS YOU CAN WHENEVER YOU CAN!

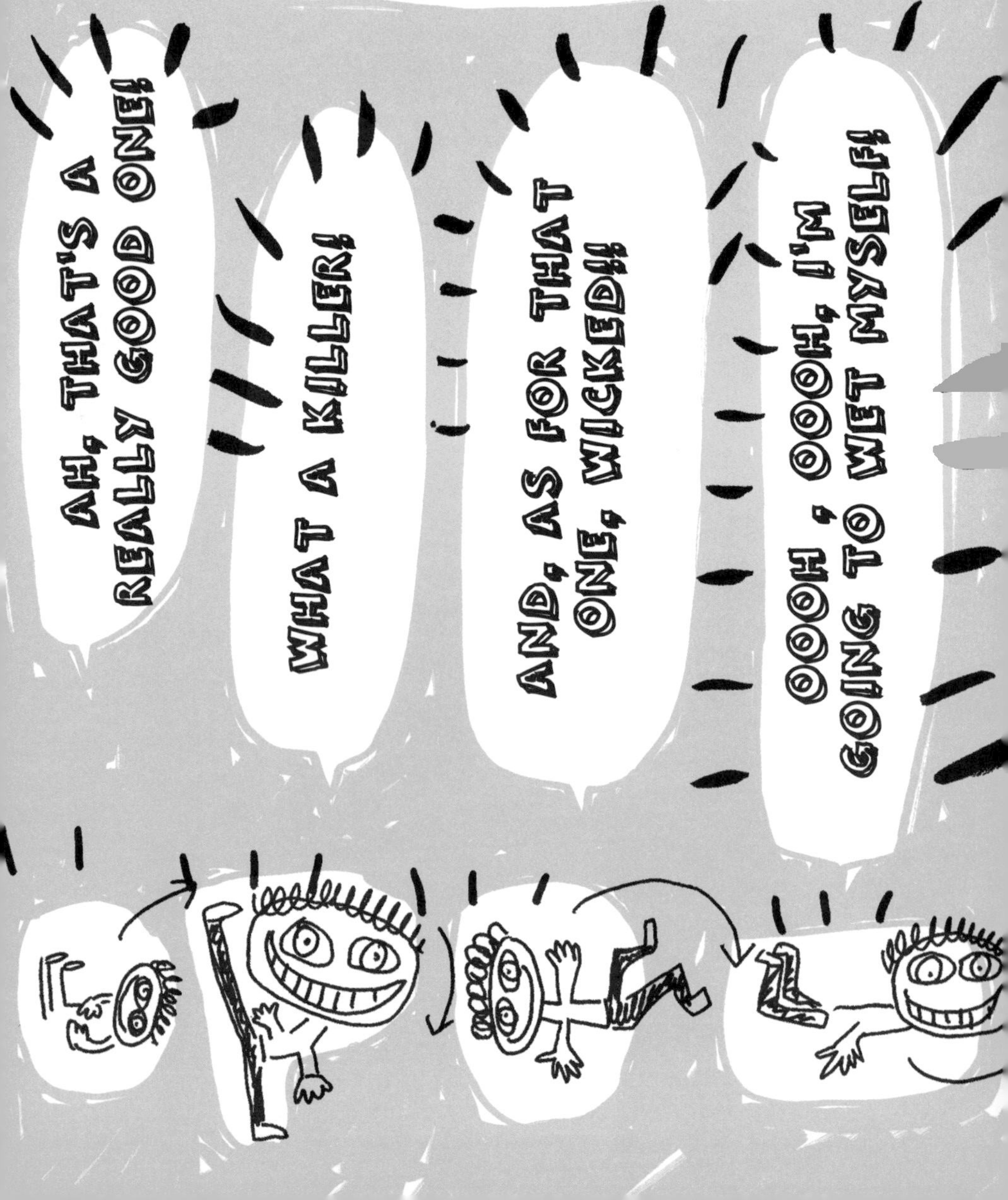

BUT PLEASE, NEVER LAUGH AT PEOPLE, IT'S REALLY NOT FUNNY.

TRY TO CHANGE THINGS FOR THE BETTER WHERE YOU CAN...

EXACTLY BETWEEN THESE 2 IS JUST PERFECT

HERE

YOU SEE, YOU CAN DO IT!

BUT ALSO ACCEPT THERE ARE THINGS YOU CAN'T CHANGE.

MISSION IMPOSSIBLE! YOU'VE GOT TO LEARN TO LIVE WITH HER!

MAKE SURE YOU'RE FIGHTING FIT ALL THE TIME.

CASE NO. 1: YOU, UNFIT

STAYING SHUT INSIDE YOUR ROOM EVERY WEEKEND

PLAYING ON THE WII EVERY NIGHT

ME? DO SPORT? NEVER!

OH DEAR... I'M SOOOOOOOOO TIRED...

LIVING ON CRISPS

WHO'S SHE???
IT'S THE FIRST TIME IN
MY LIFE I'VE EVER
OVERTAKEN SOMEONE!

GRANDAD SNAIL
TOTALLY
GOBSMACKED →

← DRIBBLES WITH AMAZEMENT

CONTAGIOUS POSITIVE VIBES

BRIGHT-EYED

CAN SPRINT AT 250 KM/H

18 HOURS OF SLEEP

TOTALLY RESISTANT TO ALL GERMS

HIGH ACHIEVER!

EATS ARTICHOKES 3 TIMES A DAY

READY FOR ANYTHING!

YUCKY SQUASHED GERM

ARGGH! WHAT A CHEEK! WHO'S THE BIONIC CREATURE THAT JUST DARED TO OVERTAKE ME?

VRRRROOOOOM VROOOOOOOM

BIG FAT SHOW-OFF IN A FERRARI

USE YOUR ENERGY WISELY. DON'T WASTE IT!

1 LIKE THIS:

NOTE: THE AUTHOR WOULD LIKE TO THANK HER CHILDREN FOR PROVIDING THE INSPIRATION FOR THIS SCENE.

ARGGGGH!!!!!!
WE'VE RUN OUT OF NUTELLA®!!!
THIS IS A NIGHTMARE!!!
WHO'S THE BRAIN-DEAD PERSON
WHO DOES THE SHOPPING
AROUND HERE????

YOUR MUM, TOTALLY EXASPERATED, READY TO ABANDON YOU AT THE LOCAL ANIMAL RESCUE CENTRE

YES! I HAVE GOT A BRAIN, YOU HORRIBLE, BAD-TEMPERED CHILD! IN FACT, FROM NOW ON DON'T CALL ME 'MUM', CALL ME 'THE BRAIN'. OK?

 A

IF YOU FOLLOW THE FANTASTIC ADVICE IN THIS BOOK EVERY DAY!

2 FINISHING LINE

HOORAY!

WOW! IT'S JUST LIKE BEING AT THE FUNFAIR!

1 START

THE GREAT HAPPINESS SPIRAL

IF YOU DO THE COMPLETE OPPOSITE:

1 START

IT SEEMS UNFAIR, BUT THAT'S LIFE!

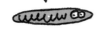

BANG

2 FINISHING LINE

THE DISASTROUS DOWNHILL SLIDE

WHENEVER YOU GET THE IMPRESSION THAT THE WORLD REALLY IS A BAD PLACE...

A BEFORE

BOO HOO!
BOO HOO HOO!
I GOT MINUS 12 OUT OF 20 IN ENGLISH...
I'M GOING TO BE BOTTOM OF THE CLASS...
I'M SO THICK....
MUM AND DAD WILL DISOWN ME...
I'LL HAVE TO RUN AWAY.
LIFE SUCKS!

FLOODS OF DESPERATE TEARS

PUT THINGS INTO PERSPECTIVE.

B ····· AFTER

> HEY, CALM DOWN!
> I HAVEN'T GOT TB.
> I'M NOT DYING OF HUNGER IN AFRICA.
> I WASN'T BORN WITH A CONJOINED TWIN SISTER
> (ASK YOUR PARENTS WHAT THIS MEANS).
> MY COUNTRY ISN'T AT WAR.
> I DON'T HAVE TO SLEEP UNDER A BRIDGE.
> I'VE GOT 100,000 MATES ON FACEBOOK AND
> I'M QUITE GOOD-LOOKING. THERE'S MORE TO
> LIFE THAN SCHOOL MARKS!

THERE YOU GO!
EVERYTHING'S FINE AGAIN!

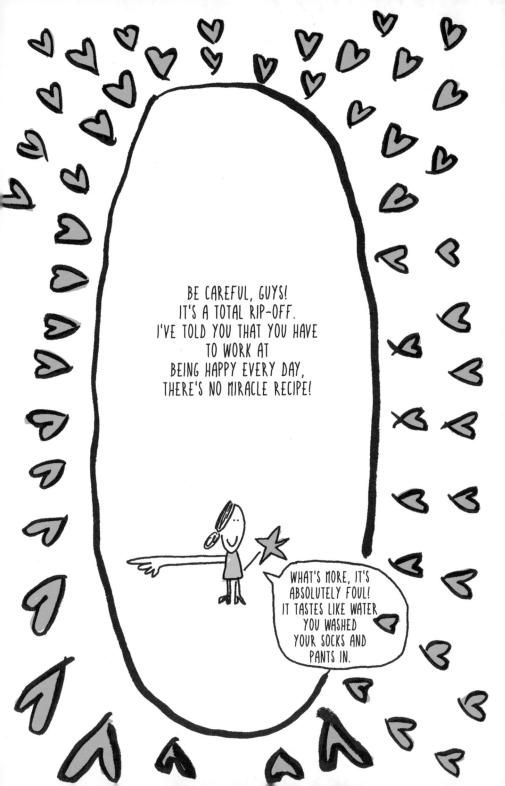

ADDED BONUS!

EXCLUSIVELY FOR YOU:
A FREE CONSULTATION WITH MIRMA, THE
GREATEST FORTUNE-TELLER IN THE WORLD!

OOOOOOOOOHHHHHHHHH!
DEAREST LITTLE READER,
I SEE A MAAAAAAAARVELLOUS,
MAAAAAAGICAL, BRIIIIIIIIIGHT
FUTURE AHEAD OF YOU!
ALL YOUR DREAMS WILL
COME TRUE!

SO DON'T WORRY,
BE HAPPY!

PERSONAL FORTUNE-TELLER TO THE PRESIDENT
OF THE USA AND HOLLYWOOD SUPERSTARS

DON'T WHINGE FOR NO REASON

(IT'S POINTLESS AND VERY TIRING).

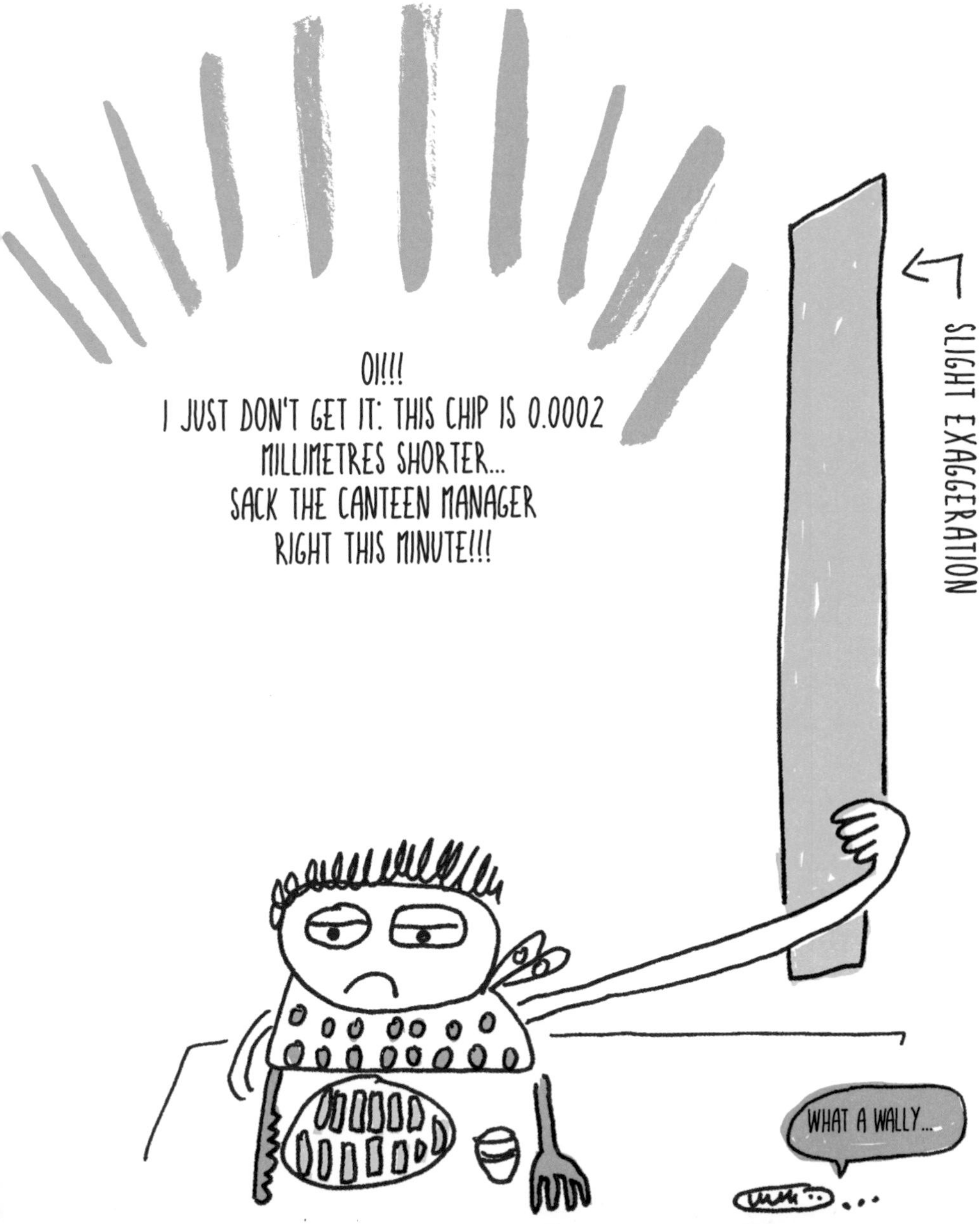

TAKE PITY ON THIS LARGE STARVING FAMILY!!

SCENARIO NO.1

YOU DON'T GIVE ANYONE A COPY OF THIS BOOK.

6 GRAINS OF RICE

MICROSCOPIC SAUSAGE TO SHARE

SCENARIO NO.2

THANKS TO YOU, THIS BOOK BECOMES AN INTERNATIONAL BEST-SELLER.

CAVIAR ALL DAY, EVERY DAY

THE AUTHOR'S FAMILY

IF, IN SPITE OF ALL THE AMAZING ADVICE IN THIS BOOK, YOU STILL CAN'T FIND HAPPINESS, TALK ABOUT IT. THE WORLD IS FULL OF SPECIALISTS WHO CAN HELP YOU.

A YOUR PARENTS

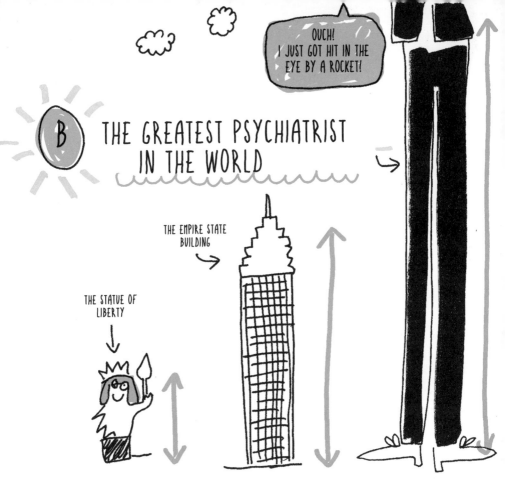

B THE GREATEST PSYCHIATRIST IN THE WORLD

C YOUR BEST FRIEND

BFF = BEST FRIEND FOREVER

THE V.B.I.! (VERY BEST IDEA!)

SHOW THIS BOOK TO YOUR MUM AND DAD BECAUSE EVERYTHING THAT MAKES CHILDREN HAPPY WORKS FOR GROWN-UPS TOO!

HAPPY PARENTS

MELTDOWN ~~X~~
PSYCHIATRIST ~~X~~
SORROW ~~X~~
STRESS ~~X~~
MEDICINE ~~X~~
SPECIAL DIET ~~X~~
TIREDNESS ~~X~~
DEPRESSION ~~X~~
PREMATURE AGEING ~~X~~
ANGUISH ~~X~~
PERSONAL TRAINER ~~X~~

IN THE BIN!

 HAPPY DOG

 WOOF!

SUPER HAPPY FAMILY!

HAPPY ENDING

SEE YOU VERY SOON! FRANÇOIZE

Published 2014 by A & C Black, an imprint of
Bloomsbury Publishing Plc
50 Bedford Square, London, WC1B 3DP

www.bloomsbury.com

Copyright © 2013 by Editions Nathan, Paris, France.
Original edition: Le livre qui te rend super méga heureux

Translated by Gillian Williams

ISBN 978-1-4729-0471-3

Printed in China

Publisher, Nathan: Jean-Christophe Fournier
Design: Albane Rouget
Production: Lucile Davesnes-Germaine
Photogravure: Axiome

10 9 8 7 6 5 4 3 2 1